Black Was Not A Label

A Collection

T0152663

ISBN 978-1-63628-099-8 (tradepaper)

Names: Ross, Kathryn H., 1993– author.
Title: Black was not a label: a collection / Kathryn H. Ross.
Description: Second edition. | Pasadena: Red Hen Press, [2022]
Identifiers: LCCN 2022039459 (print) | LCCN 2022039460 (ebook) | ISBN
    9781636280998 (paperback) | ISBN 9781636281001 (ebook)
Subjects: LCSH: Ross, Kathryn H., 1993– | African American women—
Biography
    | African Americans—Race identity | Race—Religious
    Aspects—Christianity
Classification: LCC E185.86 .R66 2022 (print) | LCC E185.86 (ebook) | DDC
    305.48/896073—dc23/eng/20221018
LC record available at https://lccn.loc.gov/2022039459
LC ebook record available at https://lccn.loc.gov/2022039460

The National Endowment for the Arts, the Los Angeles County Arts
Commission, the Ahmanson Foundation, the Dwight Stuart Youth Fund,
the Max Factor Family Foundation, the Pasadena Tournament of Roses
Foundation, the Pasadena Arts & Culture Commission and the City of
Pasadena Cultural Affairs Division, the City of Los Angeles Department of
Cultural Affairs, the Audrey & Sydney Irmas Charitable Foundation, the
Kinder Morgan Foundation, the Meta & George Rosenberg Foundation,
the Allergan Foundation, the Riordan Foundation, Amazon Literary
Partnership, and the Mara W. Breech Foundation partially support Red
Hen Press.

Second Edition
Published by Red Hen Press
www.redhen.org

This collection is dedicated to my parents, Tonya and James, who made me out of, cover me with, and remind me always to love.

To my grandmothers, Mary Helen and Rosa, who have shown me that the trauma, resilience, beauty, and grace of Black women comes in all shades of brown.

To my sister, Rosemary, who took the first step with her hair and inspired me.

To Michael D. Clark, my fearless editor and fierce friend.

To the One who first broke me open and let this spill out.

To the One who found me lovely and made it known.

To Pronto, for giving this child its first home.

And to Christ, who gave me a voice and is forever calling it forth.

Table of Contents

"Dark am I, yet lovely,"
— *Song of Songs 1:5*

Black Was Not A Label

A Collection

Ghost World 3 – Disillusionment[1]

All my life, I have lived in this brown body. Skin once fresh and new, smelling of newborn fire, has been washed, burned, dirtied, pained, adorned, loved. I speak now from this single body, both living and remembering, trying to reconcile understanding. Every memory has been imprinted into my flesh, bound up with my soul.

But here on the other side I am a ghost. I am moaning spirit straining to make sense of who I was, who I am now, and who I will be. Resignation rests like a soft, flightless bird gently cooing in my hands with its eyes on a sky it will never reach. Disillusionment is a rigid corpse in my heart, the remains of some soaring thing that fell suddenly from the blue and landed, hard, on the concrete. In its last few moments it saw visions of where it once flew—the blinding sun, the thick, fleecy clouds, the endless sea of wind and sound, and all that rested below.

I am a ghost looking at a world I once knew, another I'll never know, and a third not yet materialized.

"I know there's nothing I can do."

I am a ghost; wayward spirit clinging to nothing but the robes of Father God. I feel Him firm beside me: the only real thing.

***

What is the difference between resignation and the disappointment that comes when your reality shifts and the normal you knew is not the normal that is? A

---

[1] An earlier version of this piece appears in *The Amethyst Review*, published in May 2018. Web. Archived.

woman I respect asked me what my resignation looks like, what it feels like, and all I could say was,

"I know there's nothing I can do."

I try to detangle the two in my mind to see where resignation slips into disillusionment and back again. I type the words into a search engine and the results tell me they are different, but also the same:

[dis·il·lu·sion·ment]

noun

1. *a feeling of disappointment resulting from the discovery that something is not as good as one believed it to be.*

--

[res·ig·na·tion]

noun

1. *the acceptance of something undesirable but inevitable. To step down with compliance, passivity.*

I see both definitions within me. I see all the words I didn't say, all the times I was angry and didn't express it, all the tears I kept inside. Each word attaches itself to my body, stands stark against my skin like a tattoo, places a lens in front of my eyes. I am one and the other; I am both at the same time.

I've been told I am a miracle.
I know that I am a miracle.
All of me—sinews and muscle, blood and

bone and spirit—is a miracle.

I've been told that the Black body (my body), the Black family (my family), and the Black soul (my soul), should be cherished. That after all the Black body and the Black family and the Black spirit have been through, it is a wonder that we still rise[2], still persist. But there is a large part of me stuck in the mire that made us miracle. I am waist-deep in the swamp of slavery: the whip, the bit, rape, murder. At times I am sinking in the small comfort that I, my body, just narrowly escaped this trauma turned to testimony. But there is still pain, and still evil, and still mess and muck and mud the world throws at God, at His children.

There is still evil great and small—Black bodies gunned down, fear spread that Black bodies bring harm and so deserve harm, words and systems made weapons against Blackness—propaganda that destroys the Black body and mind from the inside out.

But even still, I know the existence of the Black person, of Black culture, is a testament to the tradition of perseverance carried in each of our bodies, in each of our souls. It is something woven into the DNA, a remembrance of those before and those to come. Even still I know that there was a time, and is a time, and will be a time when the Black body teeters close to being wiped from the face of this earth—and maybe soon to follow, every other brown body, brown family, brown soul.

I look to God and ask why—why can't miracle come from miracle?

---

[2] See Maya Angelou's poem, "And Still I Rise" (1978)

***

There is a tug towards whiteness in this world—a collective understanding that fairer is better—and this divides even brown people. It says there are *Black* and *brown,* reminding me of the schism I have experienced throughout my life, telling me that while I am brown-skinned, I am *Black.* That there is more to it than just the color—that the color doesn't dictate the culture, but the culture dictates the color.

I think of the genocide around and within us, the message that tells us—has told us—that we are not allowed to exist. We are pushed to the fringes of society, of the earth, in hopes that we might fall into the sky—blackbirds taking flight from nothing to nothing. And then, in some happy accident, the lesser brown plague might follow us unto sky, past the atmosphere, until the world is cleansed white.

Do I go too far? Or is my disillusionment just too great? Is there a middle ground where I, in my body, can dwell?

I revolve around the question, perhaps never to reach some center or understanding. I said, "I know there's nothing I can do," but this is not helplessness. It is weight. I sit constant beneath the knowledge that there is little to be done—that to try would be to strain against centuries upon centuries of strivings turned to death turned to mourning turned to moaning ghosts hurling their laments from the broken boughs of ancient trees.

When I spoke, I felt something chip away inside, fall through the empty space of my body and settle somewhere at the bottom of my soul, the floor of my understanding, like sand in water. Every now and again the sand is disturbed, kicked up by some force of hope, some serendipitous happening that whispers maybe things are as good as I once believed—maybe even better. The sand swirls and floats, turning clear water cloudy, and for a moment I can't see what I know is true. For a moment, I think it might settle into a new configuration, revealing a new truth that offers some middle ground—some compromise that tells me something is not *better* or *as good* but just *good*.

But the sand settles and the water clears, and everything is as I thought it was. As I hoped it wasn't. I look at the landscape, this wasteland at the base of the ocean of my self, and I no longer feel pain in the same way. I sit in the sand, the water swirling around me like the spirits in their gossamer shrouds. I close my eyes and think about what truth is, about what I cannot change, about what I would not change:

I am Black I am Black I am Black I am Black I am Black...

I am suddenly so tired, weighed down by the exhaustion held in the bones and flesh and heart of every ancestor, every brown-skinned body I ever was or will be connected to. It swoops upon me like a bird of prey. The words continue to unravel slowly in my mind—I see them drifting away, letter by letter out into the eddying sea until they dissolve into nothing.

The sand lays flat beneath me, gently swaying in the current, and as I breathe, I breathe in the letters, the sentences, the words, the ghosts.

I look up and see a light at the top of the water—a bright spot in the clear blue of my self. I see

God. Sometimes God is weeping, sometimes He is not. I still cannot tell if He is weeping for all of us all at once or just for me.

I send Him a question, a pulsing heartbeat that disturbs the water, momentarily stirs up the sand. I ask Him why it has to be this way, why there is nothing I can do. His light flickers and the sand settles, showing me everything as it always was, as I always hoped it wasn't.

I ask Him what this means, what He's trying to tell me, what He wants and intends for this life. I ask Him, my voice bubbling up like a jetstream, to please just make everything clear. And I beg Him, asking that if everything can't be clear to please just give me His peace as I wait for His miracle.

Defiance[3]

Standing in the middle of the bathroom I could see myself from three angles: left, right, and back. I laid a large towel down on the cool tile and then went to run my hairbrush under the faucet until it was dripping. Taking the wet brush in one hand, I undid my bun with the other and let my hair fall around me—well, fall as best it could. I ended up looking like Edward Scissorhands with my stubborn curls sticking out in all directions. Nervous excitement brewed in my stomach as I ran the wet brush over my head and watched as my wild hair began to lay flat and become heavy with moisture.

In a fit of impatience, I wrenched open the shower door, turned on the water, and thrust my head into the spray until I could feel the water running over my scalp and neck. When it was good and soaked, I stopped the shower and stepped back in front of the mirror. With one hand I began wringing out my hair and with the other I took up the black scissors resting on the counter. I exhaled steadily as I held up a thick group of strands in my trembling fingers, opened the jaws of the scissors, and sliced the blades across my hair, releasing the wet locks from my head forever.

***

The AP tests I'd taken in high school had paid off and landed me, just a freshman, in an upper division English class with nothing but juniors and seniors as my fellow students. The instructor, Professor Cook, was ancient in mind if not in body, and he spoke with

[3] An earlier version of this piece is archived in *Neutrons, Protons: A Journal of Literary Humor and Comics*, 2014. Web. Archived.

a thick accent that was hard to decipher. Perhaps Irish? Maybe Scottish. I spent most of the semester trying to figure it out, among other things. The class had been reading a short story by W.E.B. Du Bois as we worked our way through the scant literary additions of African Americans to "American Lit Since 1865." Each class we spent on the subject was torture. Professor Cook constantly veered away from the actual literature and instead focused on ethnicity and some of the worst instances of blatant racism against Blacks that ever occurred in the so-called civilized nation of the United States. My classmates did not hesitate to offer their two cents on a subject they, quite apparently, did not fully appreciate. I, however, never spoke up when we took these detours because I knew that what I was saying wouldn't be heard and my opinions would never be challenged or engaged. My skin was the only thing the other students would pay attention to, and they had already made it clear that unnecessary guilt lay upon all of their shoulders. I wished they could understand that by treating me like a victim, they were in fact victimizing me. It didn't help that the only other Black student in class didn't show up enough to split the attention and questioning I received from Professor Cook based on his perceptions of Blackness and Black experience.

During that class, we read aloud from the thousand-plus page volume of "concise" American literature. A discussion had ignited amongst the students about the treatment of Blacks after the Emancipation Proclamation was enacted. Every time an opinion was voiced, the student who had spoken conveniently skated over the defining word of the Du Bois' text. Professor Cook watched them steadily, wearing an unnerving smile. In one hand he held a Bible marked with so many post-it notes and tabs that one would think the good book had been the victim of a paintball attack. In the other he held the volume of *Concise American Literature* spread open to Du Bois' words. His eyes roved around the students and his smile widened.

"None of you will say it, will you?"

I tensed up. I couldn't decide whether to look him in the face or keep my eyes on my desk. Both options would catch his attention, which I desperately wanted to avoid.

As he waited, the class remained quiet and some students were even frowning, creases between their eyebrows indicating a level of strain that went far beyond the academic. It almost felt ironic when I thought of the dark bodies in Du Bois' story, how they picked and lifted and fetched and ran and bowed again and again to the oppression that rested around them like some malevolent spirit. Did my classmates feel this same weight? Could they? I could have sworn that some of them shot furtive glances in my direction, and each time my heart quickened as I wished to disappear completely from view.

"I'll ask you again. What did the whites call the Blacks? What did the Blacks refer to themselves as without even batting an eye? Mr. Du Bois paints a clear picture here."

Silence. Professor Cook gave us all a pitying look, then turned to me, his smile widening.

"Kathryn?"

I looked into his withered face; a lump slid

heavily into my throat.

"What about you? They called the Blacks—?"

"Niggers."

***

"Who would've thought we have so much in common? This is amazing. I can't believe we didn't meet until now!"

"I know! I used to see you around all the time, but I never imagined we'd talk."

"Why not?"

We were sitting at The Table—an unspoken haven and reprieve in the middle of long day of classes and draining socialization. My friends often said it was a place where anyone was welcome, a statement that felt like it held significant weight in high school. When other students came by at lunch, people who didn't normally hang around with us, we welcomed them into the fold, smooshing together to make sure there was enough space on the woven metal benches for everyone. The one hour of freedom we had each day was spent here—myself and my friends sitting in a circle or lounging in the grass washed in the shade of a weathered tree some of us had carved our names into.

The newest addition to our group sat beside me at the Table, arms crossed as he leaned forward, smiling good-naturedly at me. The rest of our friends lounged in the shaded grass just behind us. It was a nice cool day: the sun was out and the sky was laced with a few fleecy gray clouds like pulled cotton. Remnants of summer were still stubbornly morphing into fall, and school was finally hitting that stride of normalcy between the anxiety of the first weeks and the fatigue of a full-blown semester.

"Why didn't you think we'd talk?" he repeated. There was a smile in his eyes mingled with a look of concern. I shrugged and looked at my lap.

"I don't know…I guess what I mean is, you always looked like a cool person to talk to, but I didn't think I'd get the chance. It wasn't like our paths were going to cross…we've never had any of the same classes, you know?"

He frowned in agreement. "I suppose that's true, but I'm glad I ended up over here. I needed a change."

I nodded and silence settled between us. I shifted in my seat and he glanced at the group in the grass.

"I really am glad you're with us though," I said. He turned back to me smiling. "I can't even imagine not knowing you now."

"I feel the same," he said. "I mean, I never thought I'd have a Black friend, and here we are getting along like nothing!"

My breath caught in my throat as I looked back at him—still smiling at me like an older brother at his kid sister. The moment seemed to stretch and vanish at once; I felt wrong-footed yet unsurprised, somehow shocked by something so familiar. He was smiling still, but his smile quickly faltered.

"What?"

***

"After the Egyptian and Indian, the Greek and Ro-man, the Teuton and Mongolian, the Negro is a sort of seventh son, born with a veil, and gifted with second-sight in this Ameri-

11

can world, —a world which yields him no true self-consciousness, but only lets him see himself through the revelation of the other world. It is a peculiar sensation, this double-consciousness, this sense of always looking at one's self through the eyes of others, of measuring one by the tape of a world that looks on in amused contempt and pity. One ever feels his two-ness... two warring ideals in one dark body, whose dogged strength alone keeps it from being torn asunder." [4]

What is it to feel less than a person,
less than human, and yet still want
the other side to accept you as you are?
For I am not a *Negro*,
nor am I an *American*;
I am a believer,
a woman,
a writer,
a human being
merely presented to the world
in umber skin with a crown
of coils adorning my head.
But what differences are these really,
when humanity is set under
the eyes of God?

***

You can't be all *Black with that hair. What else are you?*
     Snip.
Is that really all yours? I mean your hair is really pretty for a Black person. No offense.
     Snip.

---

[4] W.E.B. Du Bois introduces the "double consciousness" in Chapter 1 of his essay collection, *The Souls of Black Folk*.

It's so nice like a weave! …Is it a weave?

Snip.

Let me touch it! This can't be real.

Snip.

I heard that weaves don't blow in the wind. I've noticed your hair doesn't blow in the wind. Is that a coincidence?

Snip.

Wow, do you wash it every day? Can you?

Snip.

You're lucky there are products out there that can get your hair like normal peoples'.

Snip.

Half of my head was crowned in sopping tangles while the other half looked like freshly cut grass that was shining and curling in the fluorescent bathroom lighting. The fear was gone and as I continued to cut, a weightlessness spread through me. The blades of the scissors whispered around me as they snapped at my damp hair, and with each metallic bite the soft caress of dead hair followed like the gentlest touch of someone afraid to leave the warmth of their skin on yours. The freed strands drifted away, settling in tender, lifeless piles at my feet.

Each blow of the scissors erased one of the idiotic questions I had heard throughout my life and I rejoiced because I knew I would never hear them again. It didn't matter that I'd never worn a weave, that my hair was my own, that I had loved it, once. It didn't matter that I answered their questions, my soul wilting each time I did so. There were always more, and I was always a question—a curiosity. There wasn't enough strength in me to carry it any longer, and with my scissors I cut the ties section by section.

Each time a clump of hair hit the bathroom floor, a memory of superficial but all-too-real agony vanished. The biggest fear that had lain on my heart had fluttered away only minutes after I began cutting: *what if I didn't like it?* But I loved it, and I began to cut more vigorously the further I went, shearing away old burdens I thought I had long left behind.

***

Professor Cook smiled.

"Very good," he said, and began to pace. I could feel the other students looking at me, but I didn't dare return their gaze. Instead, I stared at the textbook without really seeing it. My cheeks burned and my vision blurred, though I couldn't understand why just then. Looking back, I think it was shame.

"You were all so afraid to say that word, but it is a part of history and *this* literature," Professor Cook shook the book at the class. "You will have to grapple with how this makes you feel, but you must remember it is a part of your history, and mine." I glanced up to see him looking at me steadily before turning away. "When we read these stories, we are to say *every word* that comes under our eyes, understand?"

There was a murmur of half-hearted agreement. I sank down in my chair and checked my phone for the time. There were thirty or so minutes more to sit through.

"Now, let us continue," Professor Cook said from somewhere ahead of me. "Who will read the next passage? Mr. Du Bois isn't finished with us yet."

***

"A Black friend?" I said, answering his confused smile with a sad one. My first thought was to not look angry, to not even feel it. I didn't want to give the impression that I was offended, even if his words had shocked me. It wasn't like I hadn't heard them before from others, but I was always surprised when they were uttered. He was sitting there watching me, his eyes wide like a child who's just been caught doing something they know they shouldn't. But there was more in his expression—a nervousness in his smile, a furrowing of his brows that displayed an innocent ignorance. When he spoke, his voice was light, careful.

"Well, yeah," he said. "I mean you're Black, and we're friends and—*what?*"

In spite of myself I started to laugh, and in that moment, it felt as if I'd taken the tension in my hands and snapped it clean in two. It was always the same no matter who I met or how we got on. This was who I was to them and I would stay that way unless I actively changed their perception. Deep within me I felt this burden, but I told myself it was one worth holding if I could change just one person's mind. It was like the small strain you might feel when carrying a bag or a book—heavy but valuable, something you ought to keep with you because it is important, necessary.

He no longer looked concerned but was now smiling along with me, his face just a little unsure. "What did I say?"

Steeling myself, I looked at the sky and took a quick breath. The next few words were like wires beneath a blade—they needed care and precision, patience and a steady hand. What did it matter if a single slip could lead to the implosion of a new and budding friendship? More than I would like to admit, than I could understand just then. I felt myself swallow a lump, heavy and large like a thick, chalky pill.

I turned back to him and said, in a tone as careful and kind as I could muster, "Can't I just be your friend Kathryn? You don't know any other Kathryn Rosses, do you?"

He blinked, and looked away from me for just a moment, raking his hand through his hair. "No, I don't know any other Kathryns."

I forced another smile and looked into his face the way my mother does to me when she knows I'm worrying. Reassurance, calm. I wanted to press these feelings into him, take away any discomfort and drape it around myself instead. After all, I could hold it—have held it—will surely hold it again. But why didn't I want him to feel bad? Why didn't I want him to hurt a little, like I was? Why did I have to be the one always labeled a *Black friend* rather than a friend? I knew he hadn't meant any harm—hadn't meant to force me between patience and pain, personhood and priority—but neither had anyone else.

"See," I said, "when I look at you, I don't really see your race before you." He watched me as I spoke, and I could almost feel his discomfort rising from him in waves. I smiled again and gently touched his arm— *it's okay, it's okay.* "I just see my friend," I went on, careful to keep my voice casual and my face soft, "because you're the only you I know. Your race doesn't mean anything to me—and mine shouldn't mean anything to you."

"It doesn't! I didn't mean it that way, honest—"

I shook my head and gave him a pitying look. This was clearly more uncomfortable for him than for me—I mean, I'd been here before. I had practice with this conversation and scenario. It was second nature to expect remarks like this, but not without a twinge of shock, a sudden catching of the breath when they were said. It was normal to have to explain myself and my being, to assure the offending party that no offense had actually been made—that despite whatever they'd said, my priority was to take advantage of a teachable moment and make sure they didn't go on feeling badly about it because I was okay—*really*. This poor guy was simply floundering, choking on the foot he had so carelessly shoved into his mouth. I smiled reassuringly before speaking again.

"Look, I know you didn't mean it that way—I do—but that's what you said. Understand?"

He stared. I sighed.

"When you tack race on like that," I said, "it's like you see me as a Black person before you see me as a person. I just want you to see me as a person—your friend—and nothing else. Get me?"

"I didn't realize it sounded that way," he muttered, eyes downcast.

I waved his words away and gave him a gentle nudge with my elbow. "No one ever realizes it sounds that way. I'm used to it, but I'm not above getting preachy to set someone straight." I smiled once more, as kindly as I could, to let him know that I was not mad and hadn't been.

He nodded sheepishly. "You're deep Kathryn Ross. I'll never say that again."

"Good," I said, laughing. "The next person might not be so understanding."

***

"The nineteenth was the first century of human sympathy —, the age when half wonderingly we began to descry in others that transfigured spark of divinity which we call Myself; when clodhoppers and peasants, and tramps and thieves, and millionaires and—sometimes—Negroes, became throbbing souls whose warm pulsing life touched us so nearly that we half gasped with surprise, crying, 'Thou too! Hast Thou seen Sorrow and the dull waters of Hopelessness? Hast Thou known Life?'" [5]

Here.
Let me peel back this skin
that seems to stand in the way
between me and all that I might've wanted
from the world within the world in which I live.
For within this mask you'll find the familiar:
Bone.
Blood.
Flesh.
Endless eyes that compose the windows and gates
into a simply human soul.
Yes, God knew the sorrow and put it in us
and He saw the dull waters and let us
all swim.
And He gave us the hopelessness so that we
may find hope in Him.
So that we, regardless of the skin
we peel away,
may know life,

[5] See "Of Alexander Crummell," *The Souls of Black Folk* (Du Bois 155)

and engage in the elusive practice
of human sympathy.

***

A mound of black hair lay on the towel like a mass of seaweed. Weak waves and curls shrank at my feet and I felt no sympathy for the hair I had worn all my life. It wasn't mine anymore, anyway. After I cleaned up, I hurried to my room to grab a change of clothes. I didn't want to look in the mirror yet. I left the remnants of my hair on my bedroom floor still in the towel, considering the idea of burial—they deserved ceremony, to be mourned despite my detachment. This heap of hair was once my beauty, my conformity, my inherited assimilation—to be easier, tamed, managed, beautiful. There was so much care and joy, so much pain and shame in this piece of my body I had banished.

Back in the bathroom, I turned on the shower and stepped into the steam. Using the new shampoo I'd bought for natural hair, I quickly lathered up my hands and let the warm water wash over my face. Each time I ran my fingers through my head of freshly cut curls, I would laugh to myself, unable to contain just how wonderful this small but profound change felt.

A little while later I was standing in my towel before the big bathroom mirror with my eyes closed. I reached out to blindly wipe the mirror clean of any steam from the shower, and then I waited. I could feel drops of cold water running down my neck and back. Inhaling and exhaling steadily, I opened my eyes to see a batch of beautifully coiled curls hanging in my eyes. I placed my hands over my mouth to keep from crying out at the surprise, delight, and utter freedom I felt—it was like nothing I had ever experienced before. My eyes hungrily searched the intricate twists and turns of my hair and I wondered how I could ever have lived with hair that wasn't my own—even if it *was* my own.

When I was finished in the bathroom I went back into my bedroom to dress. Once I was done, I gathered my old hair in my hands and stood over the trash can. It was soft in death, but heavier than I could have anticipated—probably heavier than anyone would ever believe. I immediately appreciated the lightness of my new hair. With one last deep breath, I dropped the weight into the trash. As I turned away, I caught my reflection in a nearby mirror. The girl inside smiled widely at me, and I smiled back.

***

"I add that I who speak here am bone of the bone and flesh of the flesh of them that live within the veil." [6]

From this and these
I have transformed. The scales on my eyes
have finally fallen and I see with clarity
that is free from the pain of their ignorance
and my forced oblivion.
These scars are my skin
and these wounds are my memories.
Taking the old I have transformed into
the new. Bone of the bone, and flesh of
the flesh, I am different than I was.
For the eyes of man will always be blinded
by the barriers of the world we have created.
So, I shall look upon myself with my Father's eyes

---

[6] See "The Forethought" in *Souls of Black Folk* (Du Bois 3)

and perhaps, if anyone cares to look closely,
they might see Him within me
and the outward barriers
might finally pass away.

Erasure[7]

Waiting for her, I feel nervous. Wary. My stomach is un-settled, writhing. I cross my legs and my fingers, jiggle my foot to ground myself. I exhale, take a sip of water, and rub my arms as if I'm trying to get warm. Touch-ing my skin reminds me of my mother and I close my eyes for a moment, feeling the coldness of my hands against my arms, and the softness of my arms against my hands. Eyes still closed, I see myself in my mind's eye, dropping into the seat across from me.

Eyes opened, I look into my own face, a few years younger—seventeen or eighteen, maybe sixteen. My hair is much longer, past my shoulders; my body— smaller, shorter, thinner—like a child just barely cross-ing the boundary into adulthood. She smiles nervously, a quick twitch of the lips. I smile back at her and feel a rock in my throat. I don't want to do this, but I have to; otherwise she is always going to put herself in the back-seat of this life—demure and silent about what hurts, about what kills her.

I reach for her hand and she lets me hold it. It's cold, and for a moment we hold ice between us.

I say my name, and she locks her dark eyes on mine.

"I'm sorry."

For a moment she looks puzzled, and I recog-nize that discomfort at an apology she's feeling. That sudden sense that I do not deserve to feel hurt, that I do not deserve to bring someone down to the level

[7] An earlier version of this piece appears in *Linden Avenue Literary Journal* Issue 72, published in May 2018. Web. Archived. *Linden Avenue Literary* is a now defunct magazine (as of 2020).

of asking for my forgiveness. I am wrong for making them feel this way—for making myself feel this way. I'm wrong for getting hurt, because they didn't really mean it that way. And even if they did, why do I have to be so sensitive?

She shifts in her seat, pained. Her eyes leave mine and she almost shakes her head, almost waves off the apology as if it was a dirty phrase that should not have been spoken—should not have been instigated. I know what she is about to say, and I cut across her:

"I need you to remember, and I'm so, so sorry."

***

She doesn't say anything, but she doesn't need to just yet. I sit back a bit in my seat, my heart pounding painfully, beating itself against my sternum, and ask if she remembers the first time another person held their arm against mine.

I ask if she remembers how they shrieked at how close our skin tones were, at how near they were to being as brown as a Black person. I ask if she remembers when they said:

If my mom knew I was almost as dark as a Black person, she'd probably cry.

And you laughed with them, I tell her. You didn't say anything. I remember my heart sinking and dragging the rest of my insides to rest beneath my feet with it. How I quickly snatched my arm away, held it against me. I looked at it, at my skin, but suddenly it didn't look the same.

As I say this she looks down at her own skin—

my skin—as if she is remembering this memory we share that is hers and mine all at once. She doesn't lift her head, but still examines her arm, and I speak again:

Do you remember the second time someone held their arm against ours, comparing colors? She looks at me. I tell her: You said nothing. More shrieking and laughter. More exclamations at how dark they were getting since they were nearly as brown as me. There were words I swallowed so deep, I cannot recall them now. They melted in my stomach and turned to shame and bitterness. I don't know what I hated more—that I was not just Black, but a measuring rod, or that I was silent. Perhaps both at the same time.

I tell her this, but she already knows.

I tell her about how the third, fourth, and fiftieth times someone held their arm against mine, pulling my hand so that my arm stretched straight against theirs. I pulled myself away like a mother snatching her child from oncoming traffic. I cradled myself while they laughed and said in as nonchalant a tone as I could manage, *You know I'm not even that dark.*

At this she looks almost sick, because she knows how often she's said those words—how often we've said them—that betraying, plaintive tone.

I ask her if she remembers how I looked away as they continued to laugh, and from somewhere above me someone said, *Oh shit, was that racist?*

She looks like she's about to cry now, but I can't stop. I wipe my own eyes and look at her, our brown face, and I want to hold her to me. I want to tell her it was okay, but I can't, because it wasn't. Her eyes are swimming, lashes slick with unshed tears. I take her hand again and say, in the softest voice I can, "Do you remember the first time I held my arm against someone else's?"

She closes her eyes and the tears are loosed, sliding quickly in arcs from her eyes and meeting at her chin before dripping onto her lap; the beginnings of rain. Crying always gives me a headache, and I feel so sorry for making her cry. She grips my hand and I squeeze back, and I say again, "Do you remember?"

She nods, her thick long hair falling forward over her shoulders. She wipes her eyes with her free hand and nods again—yes, yes, yes.

I don't need to say this out loud because she already knows. She already remembers. This one hurts her more, hurts me more, because it's so much easier to ask for forgiveness than to be asked. It's so much easier to be wrong, because then maybe I can fix it. But I didn't try to fix it.

Her voice watery, she tells me: The first time I held my arm against someone else's, I was happy to see he was darker than me. Our skin, side by side, looked like a color gradient and for once I wasn't the end of the scale.

I ask her if this meant that we were better. I ask her if it was because the darkest person wasn't me—wasn't Black? I ask her if this proved anything I couldn't say—made a point I couldn't articulate.

She shakes her head, fresh tears falling. We finish the memory of her—me—with her—my—arm against his:

Shit man, someone had said as they laughed, watching us, *you're basically Black.*

***

I hand her a tissue and tell her to use it because we're only just getting started. I keep my voice soft and gentle, but she knows now that we've started, we cannot stop until we're done.

I ask her if she remembers when I was labeled the "Black friend." How in that moment those words jarred me awake to a truth that was always present—I was unlike the others. I ask if she remembers how that label split me, how it took me from one person to another, warring inside: the desire to belong, the knowledge I couldn't.

I ask her if she remembers how I reacted before I spoke—how the way I felt crossed my face and said more than I ever dared to. I ask if she remembers how I tried to explain the ways that label made me a *Black person* when I just wanted to be a *person*. I ask if she remembers me asking if I could just be me—if my race could just not matter. I ask if she remembers, again and again, badgering her because this is where it started. She says she does. I tell her I was wrong, that I don't feel the same. She looks at me like she already knows, but the knowing only came a moment before.

***

I ask her if she remembers how, when a pale-skinned Latina asked how long it took a Black person to poop and promptly answered her own question with *nine months*, I laughed. Fully aware they were all watching, I laughed at the joke. The girl, the joker, watched me—she was poking the bear. But I was a bear so docile I might as well have been drugged; the needle stuck into my flesh by my own hand.

I ask if she remembers the first boy I thought I loved, and she almost blushes. I ask her if she remembers how that same boy told me his friends thought he had "jungle fever" because they saw him with me. I ask if she remembers how even then, I said nothing.

I ask her if she remembers a year later, when the pale mother of the brown boy who was darker than me, the boy who loved me for a little while, looked at me with a pained expression and closed her eyes as I was saying hello.

She looks away, and I say our name again.

I ask her if she remembers how embarrassed and shocked I felt. How my first thought was that I must be such a disappointment, that she must be thinking her son could like *any* girl, so why a Black one? Why one with such brown skin, such thick lips, such unruly hair? I ask if she remembers how I only watched and smiled. His mother kept her eyes closed but I kept mine on her, willing her to just look at me. *I'm not what you think,* I wanted to shout. *I'm not like them.*

I ask myself what I was trying to prove. She says she doesn't know, but we both know she's lying.

***

I ask her if she remembers sitting with the boys at lunch when they were talking about their ideal girl. I ask if she remembers how I felt when I realized the girl looked nothing like me.

I love colored eyes—they're so pretty. Yeah, but light brown eyes are so cute too. I like super long, jet black hair. Or dark brown. Yeah. Pale porcelain skin is so fucking gorgeous.

She says she felt like an alien among them. I ask her why, even then, she didn't say anything. She says she couldn't. I say that I know.

She knows what's coming next, now, because she knows this is the one that hurts the most, the one that creeps through the dark and white-knuckles my mind late at night when I lie awake and think of all the reasons why I am not enough. I want to tell her it fades, but we know it doesn't. She looks at me and there is a plea in her eyes that asks me not to do it—to skip this one because it still hurts just a little too much, cuts just a little too deeply, speaks just a little too loudly with what I sometimes still worry are vestiges of truth. I tell her it feels like a tumor inside and this is the only way to get it out.

Resignation crosses her face, but she doesn't cry.

Do you remember, I ask her, when the boy who was supposed to be our best friend broke our heart? She sits looking puzzled, but there is an inkling of understanding as well. I am finally giving it a name. For so long I tried to gloss over it, act as if it was something rude but not detrimental. I tell her not to lie to herself, to call it what it is: heartbreak.

She looks at me. Please don't say it.
But I have to.
Please don't say it out loud.
I have to.

Doesn't it suck to know all our friends are so much *prettier than you?*

She closes her eyes and I tell her how I took a

beat, quelling the instant hurt too raw to become anger, and merely blinked. She doesn't need reminding, but she lets me talk.

I tell her how I said, *That's a horrible thing to say.*

And he said, shrugging, *Well, it's true.*

I tell her how I tried to laugh. *Are you kidding?*

No. It's just true. Black girls just aren't pretty. He paused, then added: *to me.*

But you didn't have to say that.

And he shrugged, defiant, saying that it was *just the truth.*

I ask her: why didn't you scream at him when inside everything was screaming? I ask her: why did you wait to cry? Why didn't you let him see? I ask her: why didn't you do something more than just sit there and try to pretend it didn't hurt?

I ask her if she knows why, and she says that she does. She asks me if I know why, and I say, voice so quiet I can hardly hear myself, that I do. We look at each other, eyes glassy, red, bright. I say our name again, and I hold her hand, and I feel her skin, and I watch her face, and she is so beautiful that I want to cry, more than I've ever wanted to cry for anyone, for anything.

I ask her again, "Why?"

And for a moment our voices collide, spliced together as two different strands of the same DNA. We say how I didn't want anyone to think I was one of *those Black people.* I didn't want them to think I was an angry Black girl—touchy and tetchy, a snarling beast. I didn't want them to think that I was bothered—that I cared. I didn't want them to push me into a suffocating box of stereotypes. I didn't want them to think that I was ready to call every little thing racist, so much so that I ignored racism and prejudice when it was thrown in my face. I didn't want them to see me as the negative thing they all thought a Black person was.

She's talking and I'm talking, our voices merging into one clear note—a plaintive wail of explanation, a cry for understanding, a need to be heard—they became a single voice, a single howl, a single cry. I open my eyes and I am alone with my fists closed over a hand that was never really there.

"You see me as a Black person," I said once, "but can't I just be a person?"

For a moment she's there, a ghost in the chair before me. She smiles sadly and the coldness of her skin against my own chills me. I am no longer looking back; she is looking forward.

"No," she says. "You can't."

Ghost World 1 – Heritage[8]

"In all of us there is a hunger, marrow-deep, to know our heritage—to know who we are and where we have come from. Without this enriching knowledge, there is a hollow yearning. No matter what our attainments in life, there is still a vacuum, an emptiness, and the most disquieting loneliness."
— Alex Haley, author of *Roots*

For a moment after I realized I was a living breathing person, but before I grasped the full scope of that personhood, I did not know there was a veil between me and the world I was growing up in. What I mean is I had no concept of Black.

Now, there are times when I close my eyes and see brown bodies hanging in trees. Light skin to deep dark brown, ropes around their necks. And I watch them knowing it might have been me had it not been for the few decades between their births and mine. It might have been me, thin brown body, bruises under my eyes and ashen lips, head lolling stiff from a thick brown rope. The bones in my neck broken, pushing against my skin in grotesque iterations of how they're supposed to lay, how they're supposed to stand straight in the absence of the weight bowing me down since I passed through the womb.

The understanding of my Blackness came at a time when there was already a stigma attached to the word and the description in my mind. I cannot say where or when I learned this stigma, or how exactly I attached it to myself, allowed it to be attached to me.

---

[8] An earlier version of this piece appears in *Spry Literary Journal* Issue 11, published in January 2019. Web. Archived.

But I do remember that first thought of what and who I am like the sudden drop on a rollercoaster—stomach falling upwards in abrupt surprise—not wholly unpleasant, but not entirely welcome.

As I grew and learned of bat mitzvahs, quinceañaras and debuts, I felt an emptiness in my culture and my race. I thought of holidays and rites of passage held close by different cultures pitted against those attributed to Blacks—how our days are largely created from lack, or else markers of the end of some racial trauma.

We jump the broom because our marriages meant nothing while we were slaves—families were ripped apart like one might separate a litter of puppies from their mother, children spread across the country, married women raped and forced to breed to create better, stronger slaves—a worthy return on investment. We clutch Juneteenth to our chests because it is the day the white man gave us back our liberty, our humanity, yet for years afterward we were told where to drink, where to walk, where to sit, where to live. We were sprayed by hoses and hydrants, swept away like garbage in the street before rising again on weary legs, hearts pounding with fear, with stalwart resolve.

There is no question our celebrations and traditions are important and worthy, but I can't seem to reconcile their origins. We celebrate that we remained human when the world tried its hardest to make us believe we were not. *Is that not something to celebrate?* I cry and say *it is, of course it is*—but I cannot, will not, forget that for us there is no celebration just for celebration's sake.

Like freedom, all we hold was given by the hands of those with no right of ownership to begin with. Every piece of beauty, every accomplishment comes from a culture of sorrow, a code of deletion. Pain fuels this beauty, fuels art that contradicts the notion that we are not intelligent, innovative, creative. How many times have I heard the words, *The First African American* —?

But here I must take pause. Sudden and jarring like a slamming door or clap of thunder, I remember being eighteen and in college when *African American* and *Black* were no longer synonymous. The only brown body in the room, I tried to explain that I am not *African American* after being labeled as such again and again, after my professor had me say, "*Nigger*," for no other reason than I should not be afraid to say it.

The truth is my veins carry more white blood than Black—the genes all mixed together both forcefully and voluntarily. The blood of creoles in Louisiana, of the French, of white masters. The truth is I cannot tell you—ever—where I came from. I cannot tell you who *my people* are outside of this country. I cannot tell you what African province my ancestors shuffled forth from—driven like animals rather than walking straight-backed and proud. But who could walk proudly into the hull of a ship? Who could hold their head high as they crawled atop the brown body of another, before yet another brown body crawled atop them?

I remember saying that I am not *African American* because I have never known Africa. And I remember a white boy, sickly pale with flat, colored eyes, nodding at me proudly, saying that someone *finally* got it, that *African American* was only a politically correct phrase used by guilty whites, not truth. I remember looking back at him and seeing the momentary discomfort in his face as our eyes met. The disbelief I felt at his words, at his audacity to confirm my feelings and perceptions based on a politically correct technicality washed over me, but it was strangely muted; a dulled knife with just enough sharpness to sting but leave the skin unbroken. I wondered what could have spurred him to speak, to insert himself into a space where only my voice belonged. I wondered if, in his eyes, I was *the first African American* to have understood this about themselves; if I was *the first African American* to figure it out.

***

I think of the Great Sphinx. The why and when and how of the destroyed nose sits as a supposed historical mystery, but I wonder why there is any debate at all. Is it such a stretch to think that this nose, this outlier of racial evidence, might have been destroyed to hide the truth of the civilization? Brown bodies and broad features erased from history's memory until it was normal for a young Black girl to grow up and believe the Egyptians, too, were white. I think of a video in the Southern California Natural History Museum recreating what King Tutankhamun might have looked like, my dark eyes accepting his depicted milky skin, thin lips, and pointed nose as truth and fact.

I think of how this is part of our culture of sorrow: erasure of the self by the other leading to erasure of the self by the self. How else could they justify the lie that we had sub-human intelligence, sub-human souls? How else could they enslave a people whose brown-bodied brothers and sisters created and solved equations? Who aligned the Pyramids to mirror the stars?

Sometimes when I close my eyes, I still see brown bodies hanging in trees. I see brown bodies hanging in trees, heads bowed and chins reaching for chests and she whispers to me—tells me not to eat the strange fruit.[9] My mother might have worked in the house and my father in the field and my sister with my mother and myself with my father and where is my God?

I inherit rage, sorrow, deletion, death. I inherit displacement—a blind woman walking with the veil like scales over her eyes. The past is cloaked in a thick pall that has me asking what celebrations might I have inherited from *my people*? What days, what festivals, what rites of passage are lost in the silenced annals of our murky past?

***

It was not enough to see the lies or the way I swallowed them. It was not enough to feel simultaneous shame and pride in my body—the striking length, the beautiful texture of my hair, the selfsame lightness and darkness of my skin, the thick curvature of my lips, the lift of my cheek bones, the slight arc of my brown-black eyes. Who constructed this face? From where did these features come? Who handed my eyes down to my father's parents, to my father, to me? Who gave my nose, my smile, to my mother's parents, to my mother, to me? Who were the brown bodies who lay

[9] Singer Billie Holiday sings the lines, "Southern trees bear strange fruit, blood on the leaves and blood at the root, Black bodies swinging in the southern breeze, strange fruit hanging from the poplar trees" in her 1939 song, "Strange Fruit."

with other brown bodies to create my grandparents, my parents, me? Who were the white bodies forcing their way into the brown bodies, into a line that might never have known them had their ships with empty, gaping hulls remained on northern shores?

These white bodies loosened the coil in my hair, lightened the hue of my skin, left an inheritance of unmerited pride and shame in my body—pride and fear for my body. There is more white blood than Black blood in these veins. But there are strands in my DNA, woven with intention, laced with resilience and persistence. There are genetic codes buried so deeply that variations of darkened skin and coiled hair will persevere forever, shaping faces and ordering cells so that they recall the brown bodies taken from the shores, set to the fields, hung from the trees.

I am a lost daughter calling out to distant mother, calling out to Father God, asking where I ever belonged, asking who I was supposed to be.

Little Brown Girl

Little brown girl,
do not cry because, to some,
brown is synonymous with
ugly.

>Little brown girl,
>do not cry because your
>beauty comes with modifier
>and descriptor to explain, to clarify.

>>Little brown girl,
>>do not cry because they think
>>you are *exotic*, because
>>they think you are sweet—
>>*chocolate, coffee, caramel*—
>>devil's food cake.

And,
Little brown girl—please,
when you've wiped your tears—

do not ask me why.

Hair[10]

When I first wrote this, I was twenty and new.

At the moment I write this now, I will be twenty-three for two more months—somewhere between the middle of a bathroom flooded with fluorescent light, scissors in hands, and the rest of my life.

The night before I began my last year of grad school, I cut my hair for the first time in a year. In death the curls tightened, seized up like muscles in the moments before a collision and lay closely wound together like black springs. They fell with each slice of the blade like peculiar rain on the bathroom floor. The fluorescent bulbs hummed, and my brown face looked washed out, almost ashen, in the stark mirror.

The first time I ever cut my own hair was four years previous in the summer. It was longer and thinner then, flattened by heat and chemicals that straightened the springs, pulled them taut. I was nineteen then and a life I used to know was dying by my own hand.

The rain picked up, a dark downpour coating the floor in black wisps that were once washed, conditioned, moisturized, cared for. Outside it was nearly ninety degrees, 8pm. A heat wave in the last days of August baked California—a relentless heat that comes only when summer knows its days are numbered and so blazes instead of wilts, blasting the last of its flames on an already dried out world. I looked in the mirror and saw lines beneath my eyes and thought about how just an hour ago I was sitting on my bed, pulling out my hair

[10] An earlier version of this piece appears in *Burnt Pine Magazine* Issue 5, published in March 2019. Web. Archived.

strand by strand by strand like I always did, like I always do, letting it collect into a tumbleweed at my fingers. I ran my hands through it and it felt tired and dull and suffocated. I knew it was already dead. But now it is collected into black puddles at my feet and I am forced to wonder: how does drought become moisture?

When I dream about myself now, my hair is still long and straight like it was when I was a child. I think about being sixteen and braiding it at night so it would be textured in the morning. Big, thick curls that cascaded around my face and down my back. They were mine, but when they were wet, they fell straight, put in their place by the chemicals and flat iron that seared the life from them once a week, every week. I'd stay up no matter what, sick or dead tired, braiding and weaving because then maybe people would ask fewer questions. But then I cut it all off, in this same bathroom and watched the locks like clumps of seaweed wilt at my feet. My natural curls were given their first chance to breathe, finally free from the chemicals and choking heat and hands of curious strangers picking through them, detectives on an insolent, irrelevant case.

A woman's crown and glory is her hair, but mine, wound tight at the roots, sat like a garland of thorns for far too long. I remember the girls in the locker room sneaking behind me, looking at my scalp, searching for the non-existent tracks of synthetics hidden among the strands of my straightened hair, too long for them to believe its reality. It was all I was.

Why do I remember this?

At sixteen I combed my hair, felt my wiry roots unraveled and pulled straight against the teeth of the brush as it ran from scalp to tip in repeated downward motion. I felt the renewed length and softness as knots and tangles released, leaving behind a smoothness that slid, effortless, between my hands. Now, I run my fingers through the curls once, twice, three times, and watch them reach upward, breathing and thriving like stalks of spiraled wheat, baked black.

Once stretching three inches upward, my curls are now cropped close to my scalp and my head feels lighter. Dark puddles sit at my feet, not wilting but seizing and shuddering before they stagnate, lie still. Somehow softer now than when they were attached, I held the curls, like cotton, in my hands. In the mirror I still looked tired, wan. Brown face under fluorescent lighting, shadowy rain in my hands. I ran my fingers over the fresh cut and it was soft and gentle, as if it had just taken the first breath of life. It makes me think of forests sprouting from ash, my blade like fire against the dying trees that crowned and gloried my skull.

I asked my mother what she thought, and she frowned slightly like she wasn't sure. *I like it long,* she said, and I knew what she meant, even though my hair hasn't really been long in years. I told her she'll get used to it. She said it doesn't matter, so long as I like it. Except I don't know if I do. I looked at the black cotton in my hands, sheared willingly. I thought of other brown hands grabbing, shearing, plucking white cotton in wilting fields beneath a relentless sun. I looked at my own hands, where the black cotton sat soft and light in my palms, and suddenly wished it were still attached. It hasn't been long in years, but I still dream about it and wake remembering the blade releasing the locks from scalp to floor, thick rain that thunders until it stills. It hasn't been long in years, but it haunts me like a murder.

Why do I remember this?

***

It all starts with my hair. Everything, everything starts there. It starts with being seven years old, my mother standing behind me in the early morning dividing my hair into two sections and weaving them into long, thick braids. The same look every day. She would hold my chin and smooth my hair, then kiss my cheek before releasing me to the world. My second-grade teacher, Mrs. Lindsey, tall, thin, and brown with a southern accent and high, powerful cheekbones, would come up behind me and stroke my hair, tell me how much she loved it.

She was from Louisiana and, though I didn't pay attention to it then, so was my family. I have deep roots in Opelousas, a Black Creole grandmother white as silk and a grandfather brown and broad-faced with a sharp nose he gave my mother, who gave it to me, softened by my father.

If my grandmother is silk, my mother is almond milk, and I am soil mixed with water, made into mud. Mrs. Lindsey was bronze. Skin freckled and wind-burned smooth, bright brown eyes. She would call me to the front of the class while she taught math lessons and take one of my braids in one hand and a ruler in another. Pressing the edge of the ruler into my scalp, she would then pull the end of my braids gently, further extending the curls my mother had painstakingly brushed straight, and ask:

> "How long are Kathryn's braids?"
> *12 inches,* the class would answer.
> "How long is 12 inches?" she would ask.
> *A foot,* the class would answer.

She wouldn't let go of my braids but would loosen her grip just a bit. *Look how long,* she'd smile. *Look how beautiful.* I smiled back, feeling pride at the length, aware it was special—aware it set me apart. She'd let go and the braids would spring back, slowly recoiling, pulling each strand tight like hands reeling in a rope ladder or a fishing line.

It starts with being nine, sitting under the dryer with a *Harry Potter* book in my hands, waiting for my curls to release the moisture they had drunk deep into themselves during my sink wash. My mother would place a mat on the counter and I would lie back into the basin, neck bent against a towel, while she shampooed and conditioned and rinsed. She'd wrap a towel around my hair and sit me up, help me down, and walk me over to the chair where I would spend the next five or six hours while she blow-dried, brushed, and braided and I cried and cried and cried.

Everyone said I was a tendered-headed crybaby. A wailing banshee with the wet hair of a witch. Even then I knew they weren't wrong, but it didn't change anything. Each stroke of the brush unraveling the corkscrew curls twisting up from my scalp felt like my skin being ripped apart. Section by section, thin braids trailing down my back that pinched as my mother wove the strands over and across the others. She'd string beads at the ends so that they clicked together while I walked or ran. My mother, exhausted, always said I had so much hair. She gave up Saturday nights and Sunday afternoons to care for it, to braid it, to adorn it with these small shining beads like jewels. The little girls in my class would run their fingers through it, wishing they, too, had trinkets in their hair, unable to understand what those trinkets cost.

It starts with being eleven, hair past my shoulders in a straight, chemically altered sheet. Long and beautiful like it had always been, still shown the same amount of care if not more—but *easier*, now. Managed.

I was so ashamed for so long.

Was there shame in saying your hair needed help to be worn every day? No more break-neck brushing, no more crying? There was when the girls who surrounded you had hair that grew long and straight, flowed like water from the faucet. There was when these girls touched and fondled your hair, examined it for authenticity, forever an anomaly. Still thick, despite the chemicals. Still growing. There was when you were questioned, when being Black wasn't explanation enough for the length, because "just Black" girls didn't look like that.

My mother still guided me up to the sink, neck bent against the towel, head in the basin. Shampoo, condition, rinse, dry. She'd sit me in the same chair and run the flat iron from root to tip, root to tip, over and over again until my entire head was sleek and shining, soft and flowing. Saturday afternoons and Sunday evenings—who was I to feel shame in the face of such care?

A small Indian boy would make eyes at me as I sat alone on the concrete in the early morning hours before school, head bent over a book so that my sheet flowed around me like a shroud. I would glance at him and smile, but his eyes were always on my hair.

A small mixed girl would offer back-handed compliments, corner me in homeroom to ask how I got my hair like that, how it was possible, if she could touch. She would tell me I was beautiful. But like him, her eyes were always on my hair, traveling from root to tip with a ravenous scorn, a veiled disbelief. *You're so pretty.*

It starts with being fifteen, having fallen into a rhythm. Wash, dry, straighten—once a week, every week. I learned to wash and straighten on my own, staring into the bathroom mirror as I divided sections, ran the flat iron from root to tip, root to tip. A trip to the salon every three months, sitting in the chair with a burning chemical paste at my roots, smoothing out the new growth. My hairdresser would take a comb and rake it across the curls, loosening them and loosening them until my hair dropped another inch or two.

When I left, my hair was plastered to my head. Flattened, thinned. I began to schedule these salon trips during school breaks so I had days to recover, so no one would notice enough to ask.

It starts with being sixteen, and then seventeen, and then eighteen, and friends asking why my roots didn't match my curls. Sitting up night after night, brushing and braiding and twisting, just to feel normal in the morning. Compliments when it was straightened, long and silky. Questions when it was curled, thick and frizzy. Suspicions that it was all a big fake. Why the hell did anyone even care?

It ends with a fevered summer and scissors and then—invisibility. No more questions. No more touching, no more investigations. No more comments about not being Black enough, a closet mulatto. Suddenly, I was too ethnic to be seen.

In the World Where I Do Not Exist[11]

"In another world, you could be white."

He stares at me, and I stare back. And we say nothing.

"But then, it wouldn't be you," he finishes, his voice softer. His eyes, no longer on me, look out ahead of him, as if he sees her, the me that isn't me, and I wonder what I, *she*, looks like.

Maybe her skin is pale and her hair is long and perhaps golden like the girls all men love even if they say they don't. Her eyes are probably blue and her hair straight, saved from the violent curl God gave me as some cruel, sick joke.

Except, I don't think it was a joke or cruelty. And I don't think there is another me anywhere, in this or any other world. I am here, only. My soul cannot occupy two spaces in time, but he wants it to. Because, he may not choose me, but he would choose her. She is safe, and she is pale, and her eyes are not black holes, which makes her beautiful.

I look at him and shrug. "Maybe."

Does this sound familiar? Do you remember it?

He looks at me again, but his eyes are different, and I'm

[11] An earlier version of this piece appears in *Split Lip Magazine*, published in October 2016. Web. Archived.

so sure he's wishing I was in that other world, and the other me was here in this world, sitting with him beneath the wide winter sky, dappled light spilling over us, casting shadows. Her skin wouldn't absorb the sun, but reflect it, and she would be beautiful in a way I am not.

If he asks if this is about him, I'll lie.

I should get up and leave, but something holds me here. Part of it is shame, the other part something less definable. Because, I would be lying if I said that, at some point in time, I hadn't stood in front of the mirror hating what I saw. It would be the deepest of self-deceptions to say I never hoped I would wake up different, freed from this *ugly brown cage* the world told me was not, *could not*, be beautiful. I would be lying if I said I never protested the darkness of my skin, said *it's not* that *dark*, in an effort to make myself feel better, validated, whole.

If he asks if I cried while I wrote this, I'll lie.

***

I told my mother once that I was ugly. Told her I was sure of it because the boys at school didn't like me. They made fun of my hair and my lips, of the food I ate, and the deep darkness of my skin. The children asked questions that made me feel less than human— Could my hair be washed like a "normal person?" Did *my people* eat anything besides fried chicken? —and I answered like a fool, trying to prove I was a person, entire and complete despite the differences.

But real people don't have to prove that they are real.

They just are, and the universe acknowledges the space they occupy.

> *"Jesus loves the little children, all the children of the world. Red and yellow, black and white, they are precious in his sight…"* [12]

They changed the lyrics before I left the elementary school. Someone somewhere realized that, *maybe*, those lyrics were *a little* racist, or, at the very least, *a little* dangerous if anyone ever questioned them. We never did. The principal himself stood ahead of the school during chapel, hands held aloft as he taught us the new words to sing,

> *"Every color,* dark to light, *they are precious in his sight, Jesus loves the little children of the world…"*

But even then, I knew that across the spectrum, love varied depending upon if you were *dark or light.*

***

The air is barely settling, still disturbed by his words, the timbre of his voice: *In another world, you could be white.* Hardly any time has passed, but it feels like we've travelled miles. I stare at him as he stares somewhere beyond us and I can't shake the feeling that I am not right. That he has, perhaps accidentally, revealed that because of what I am not, we will never be.

If he asks if I love him, I'll lie.

[12] Lyrics from the hymn, "Jesus Loves the Little Children." The music was written in 1864 by George Frederick Root as a Civil War song titled "Tramp, Tramp, Tramp, the Boys are Marching," and the words were written for the tune later by Clare Herbert Woolston, who was inspired by Matthew 19:14.

I think of the other me in the other universe and I wonder if she is happy. I wonder if she feels beautiful because her skin is light and her hair is thin and her eyes are reflecting pools that men want to get lost in, not black holes that will suck them in and never let them go. I think of her, someone I have never thought of, and wonder why this is the moment we see each other for the first time. Has she always been there, watching? Has she always been hovering on the fringes of my universe? Or is this the moment she was called into existence—made real from the negative space of all I am not—all I can never be.

***

My great-grandmother told my grandfather to lighten up the race. She was not the only brown mother who told her brown son that a woman was only worth loving if her skin looked like milk and her hair grew down and long, not up and out. She was not the only brown grandmother who wanted to exchange her brown grandchildren, who wanted to bring the grandchildren from the *other world*, the light ones with light eyes and loose hair, and make them wholly, truly her own.

I wonder if my grandfather wondered. Did he ask himself, *Then who loved you?* Did he ask himself, *Then who will love me?* (And I ask myself, *Who will love me?*) Great-grandmother was brown and he was brown, and yet she had been loved, hadn't she? But he listened— and produced three children *dark to light*.

Am I dark? Are you, in every world of your multiverse, light? Would I be better if I stayed out of the sun?

It wouldn't matter if I did. This darkness is in my *DNA*. Maybe God laughed as he wound those strands together, coiled them tight like my thick Black hair.

But I don't hear God laughing, and neither do you. I don't think you hear God at all. But maybe, as you're looking out ahead, while I sit beside you, you're asking Him why He didn't just make us right. Why did He give us the sun and this skin that drinks it in, burns and browns beneath it?

In that other world, are you there, too? Are you pale with colored eyes and goldenrod hair? Or are you something else completely? And in that world, are you wishing that the me who is beside you, looked more like the me who is here beside you now? Are you wishing she had umber skin and full lips? Are you wishing her eyes were black holes pulling you deeper? And are you wishing that when you run your hands through her hair, you'll feel the twists, turns, and spirals of those God-woven curls?

Or is there only one you, sitting beside the only one me, eyes forward, wishing, deep inside, that brown things did not exist?

If I ask him for the truth, he'll lie.

"Maybe," he says.

Addendum

I add this here as a reminder to you, reader, and to me, writer, and to me, rememberer, that I am bone of the bone, and flesh of the flesh, of these and those from within the veil. I am citizen of the veil two hundred years removed in word only. I am the 'we' I spoke of. Naïveté was smothered by word, by deed, by thought, by hand, by love given and taken and not returned. I no longer wish to peel away skin or expose bone or flesh or become vulnerable to a world and a people beyond the shackle, beyond the shroud, beyond the erasure, beyond the safety of the veil.

I huddle close to brown bodies that look and feel and weep something like mine. I cling to tan and brown and mahogany hands and wait to kiss lips and taste love on teeth that lock trauma away. *Not yet, not yet,* whispered by bitten, waiting tongues. I don't want to shut any body out. But not every body understands that my love comes with and from within the veil—clinging to my fingers, draped over my face, my eyes, my hair. I lean close and listen for whispers that seep past the teeth of those who stand within, without, besides, between the veil. I add this to remind you, reader, that I, writer, must remember, always, that I am bone of the bone and flesh of the flesh of these and those from within the veil.

Brown People

When God made me,
He held me a little too
close to the sun. He
snatched me away just
in time and blew sweet
breath to cool my burning
skin. Phaethon[13] laughed at me,
relieved that he was not the
only one who could not handle
the sun. But God watched him
as he held my cooling form in
his scarred hands. He plucked
a spiral galaxy from the void
and, multiplying its arms,
lengthening its strands,
He crowned me. Phaethon
continued to laugh. His father's
chariot held that star loosely and
he fancied himself as competent
as God. But Father kissed my
finished body. He whispered I
was *very good*. And looking
into Phaethon's eyes he said,
"I make no mistakes."

---

[13] According to Book II of *The Metamorphoses* by Ovid 24-32. In Greek my-
thology, Apollo, the sun god, would attach the sun to his chariot and pull it
across the sky throughout the day. His son, Phaethon, took over one day, lost
control, and brought the sun too close to the earth, burning the people down
below. Blackened but otherwise unharmed, the descendants of these people
have forever been dark-skinned. This story is meant to explain the existence
of brown, or "dark" people.

Ghost World 2 – Womanhood¹⁴

The cruelest thing God could have done, He did to me lovingly. Needle and thread in hand, He stitched me together, breathed into my nostrils, brought forth my first cry, and made me a Black woman.

Through the eyes He gave me, I see a genocide of brown people by brown people. A massacre turned both inward and outward, conducted most cruelly through the withholding of love, the impossibility of desire. An inferiority complex turned self-hatred turned mantra that whispers, again and again: *you are not worthy of the unconditioned, unfettered love you desire.*

This genocide begs Black and brown men and women to erase brownness in their children, their grandchildren—adding white paint until black is grey is white again. I have heard mothers tell their young brown boys and girls they are not to bring home a dark lover, a Black lover, a brown lover. I have heard voices from other branches, other roots of my familial tree say, boldly, that we need to lighten the race: *Find someone like you, but not dark.* I ask: what is dark? Is it simply anyone and everything that cannot be called light?

I wonder, had God not been so cruel, if things would be easier. If all that He placed inside of me would shine brighter, speak louder. I wonder if love would not be offered to me like scraps.

I wonder if the Black and brown men and boys who have pursued me, claimed they liked me, even

¹⁴ An earlier version of this piece appears in *Crack the Spine Literary Magazine* Issue 244, published in November 2018. Web. Archived.

loved me, would not have offered it like a favor, like I automatically owed them my attention and affection in return. They would not speak to me like I am being given something I could never earn, something I don't really deserve. I would not feel uneasy and afraid when they eyed me, would not turn my face from them, afraid to catch their eye and bracing myself for aggressive, unwanted attention that says I am already theirs because I am brown, not because I am wanted. I am a Black girl who should know her place. Intelligent, pretty even, for such brown skin. An enigma wrapped in a contradiction; an exception just worthy enough for offhand affection. Who am I to dare turn them down? What do my feelings matter when they are giving me a pass?

I wonder, had God been kinder, if light-skinned men of every race would look me in the eye. If their desire would not be masked and their feelings for a Black girl would not incite fear, shame. If seeing me as someone beautiful, someone worth knowing, would not be exotic and outlandish, a phase that would soon fade away. I wonder, had God chosen to spare me, if I could be an option—truly seen and truly wanted. Not a pass or an experiment, not a source of shame but a person—viable and whole.

I think, too, of the couples I have seen, the ones made up of molasses and ivory, honey and coal, butter and copper. I think of their smiles, the way they seem to see deep into one another, beyond the cages of different-colored flesh, and I wonder if they have found a way past the internal genocide. How have they pushed past the stigma, the fear, the assumptions, the overt prejudice so much of the world sees as normal?

I see them and think of seeing, *really seeing*, your lover, of accepting every facet of their being, every physical attribute, as a complement to the soul you have chosen to love. How did these people, these couples, fight through God's love and His cruelty and find one another? Will anyone ever find me?

***

The first time I truly and completely fell in love, I found someone like me on the inside. I found someone who knew what it is to be brown, if not the same brown as myself. I found someone who saw and cared for my soul, prescribed it no color. I found someone who did not give me worth, but saw worth long and deep within me, reminded me it was there. I found someone who never told me I was beautiful, but made the fact known in small, quiet ways that made me glow from the inside.

Love was soft and surprising, a young phoenix rising from a pile of ash, warm and small and fluttering. Vulnerable and unsure. Furtive glances and soft, careful touches. Words, transparent and shimmering, extracted from the soul and presented to one another—placed with the other where we knew they were safe. He never so much as held my hand, but once or twice held me close to him, gentle. His touch so careful I might have been spun from glass.

The first time I truly and completely fell in love, it was because someone saw me—the hidden me, stifled and ignored since I learned *brown* and the shame attached to it. Someone saw me, and I've so rarely felt seen.

This love was short-lived and sudden, a profound impact that struck me, within me, settled deep under my skin. With a whimper—a gasp—the phoenix burst back into flame. The zeal of being seen had given way to partial blindness and we unraveled, slowly at first and then all at once, coming to rest as something new but different in a way that hurt—the smallest sting.

The tears I cried for him were different than any I had cried before. Different than when, in college, a Black man old enough to be my father badgered me every day before and after our shared class to talk to him, to befriend him. He showered me with compliments, eyes wide and eager as he watched me squirm. He soon told me I was racist for not giving in, that I thought I was *too good* for a Black man, that I was wrong for *not just giving him a chance*. Different than when a white man at my first university told me I was beautiful and exotic, sat so close behind me that each of his warm breaths settled like a noose around my neck, took offense when I told him off. Different than when, in high school, the brown boy who said he loved me sent seventeen text messages detailing everything he hated about me because he couldn't have me. My presence, once a comfort, was nothing but a nuisance to him, a source of pain turned to slow-burning resentment, and I crumbled beneath his loathing. But these new tears were the keening of a wounded animal, the response to the sudden tearing, the sudden snuffing of a soft, glowing soul.

The first time I truly and completely fell in love and lost it, the phoenix reappeared, small and aching, but burning like a pilot light against the dark. Gentle and quiet, some words still extracted from the depths of the soul and shared, others held tightly in my mouth. I padded myself around him, stifled the wealth of emotion I felt for him, erected three or four inches of safety between his heart and mine.

There were shadows in the way now, ghosts moving between us I hadn't seen before.

**

Now, I think of him and how the worst thing God could have done, He did lovingly. Needle and thread in hand, He stitched him together, breathed into his nostrils, brought forth his first cry, and made him brown.

If God had spared him, would he love himself? If God hadn't been so cruel, would he need lovers with loose hair, light eyes and milk colored skin to hand him the worth he swears he doesn't have? Would he need her to tell him he matters? To echo the words that weren't enough when I said them?

What is validation and who can give it? Did he ever give it to me? Could I have ever given it to him? I look at my dark hair and eyes and skin and know the answer. I know it and for a moment I imagine the girl softly whispering worth into his ear, wrapping pale fingers around his brown hand. She makes him stronger, smarter, better; I remind him of everything he lacks. But when he talked of his pain, when he talked of the beautiful, mean world and how it hurts the brown body, didn't he speak to me?

Could he have spoken to her?

**

The first time I truly and completely fell in love,

he later told me in a voice so soft and gentle it might have been spun from glass: *in another world, you could be white.* I looked at him, the one person who saw me, the first person I have loved, and realized with a pang that maybe, just maybe, he didn't always see me, or himself, like I thought. Perhaps that what I had seen in him, and what he had seen in me might have only been the momentary glimpses of a glowing brown body, a glowing soul, freed from the ever-present genocide, the weight of not-good-enough. I thought maybe, just maybe, the genocide is alive—virulent—within him, further and deeper than I could have ever guessed.

I want to believe that small things like the darkness of one's skin, the texture and hue of their hair, or the color of their eyes do not dictate who receives love, and who does not. I want to believe lovers are not taken for what they can give or affirm, but for who they are. I want to believe that these things on the surface don't matter when souls match. I want to believe that people only take lovers because of love.

But, no matter how desperately I want to, I can't.

Within the Veil

"I who speak here am bone of the bone and flesh of the flesh of them that live within the veil." [15]

I imagine brown ancestors walking, shackled to one another at the ankles and the throat, through a veil. They are coming from blazing heat and vast skies, lush trees and the smell of creation. Man first emerged here, walked upright into blinding daylight, let the sun kiss his flesh until it was baked black, smelling of fire. *Negro*. Brown skin, black hair, dark eyes. They are going to gray skies and rough seas. To bent backs and sweating brows. To *boy, nigger, slut, missy*. Shackled to one another at the ankles and throat, piled one body on top of another like lumber stacked for maximum profit, the sons and daughters once held in the cradle of the tree of life, severed at the roots.

As they pass through the veil it does not fall back or glide over them. It clings, draping itself over their heads, against their eyes and in their mouths, obscuring their vision. They move forward, shuffling from warmth into darkness, from home into diaspora, until the veil falls over the last of them, covering every last body that was, every body that is, every body that is yet to come. They are a people who have passed through but not beyond, trapped in an endless tunnel that loops back into itself, a sepulchral labyrinth.

We are those from within the veil.

***

In some attempt at understanding what I knew

---

[15] See "The Forethought" in *Souls of Black Folk* (Du Bois 3)

myself to be, I said this—again and again—to make sense: *I am a person who happens to be Black, not a Black person.*

Black was not a label, but a vague descriptor. Something to encompass my features, my skin, my hair—at most. Whatever a Black person was, I was not, though not because I did not want to be.

I used to say that no matter what color I was, I would essentially be the same person. I would be the same person who read *Harry Potter* books, who felt most alive in the water. I would be the same person who was shy and quiet, who could not raise her voice higher than a baby yell, a shout of laughter. I would still listen to movie soundtracks and old rock n' roll. I would still love Jesus and say my prayers each night. I would still talk clearly, enunciating my words like I was taught to in the fourth grade. There was no such thing as *sounding white* or being an *Oreo*, I was just being myself, as my parents had been themselves.

In the 70s, they bonded over Elton John, James Taylor, and the Jackson 5. They played records of The Beatles and Tom Petty and the Heartbreakers which they later passed on to my sister and me. In the 80s, my father studied poetry and English, and my mother biology and nursing. My father wore an afro and a Jheri curl, my mother a press and a perm. They watched *Pee-Wee's Playhouse* on Saturday mornings in the early years of their marriage and *Martin* on Primetime. Both their families said they were a little weird—acted "white." In the early 90s, they bore my sister and myself and we heard the same things all throughout our childhood.

Within this veil, there is not room for two warring souls, for a double consciousness. Everything is or it is not. I am either *this* or another thing entirely. Within the veil everything is branded, stamped across the forehead with thick ink that reaches through the skin and into the brain, choking the synapses until they comply with the predisposed directive.

"It is a peculiar sensation, this double-consciousness, this sense of always looking at one's self through the eyes of others, of measuring one by the tape of a world that looks on in amused contempt and pity." [16]

***

There might have been a moment when the world was not split straight down the middle. A moment before the when. Where the veil fluttered momentarily and those on either side had a glimpse of what lay beyond their field of vision. From one they saw a dark people, wrapped in an inability to forget, to loosen, the past. From the other they saw a pale, muted world, covered in a fog where shapes and shadows move about like ghosts. Scales on their eyes and cloth forced into their ears, bits in their mouths, hands shackled behind backs, and souls chained to boulders, dragging them, dragging us, dragging me, down into the murky depths where the world rematerializes around us, both hazy and over-bright; stark darkness.

I hear a lone voice shouting; asking: *"Hast Thou seen Sorrow and the dull waters of Hopelessness? Hast Thou known Life?"* [17] And I sit on the corner of the Ghost Worlds, spinning themselves outward, reaching into the

---

[16] See "On Our Spiritual Strivings" in *The Souls of Black Folk* (Du Bois 9)

[17] See "Of Alexander Crummell," *The Souls of Black* Folk (Du Bois 155)

world beyond the veil—a world I'll never really know. I ask myself how long I'll stay here in the in-between, eyes watching the shadows that rest between myself and everything I've ever wanted, ever hoped for.

I ask God the Father to meet me here—ask the Son to walk me from one corner to the other— ask the Holy Ghost to touch the veil, turn it opaque so that I can at least see and then know.

I feel His hand close over mine, the gentle pull as He brings me to my feet, and guides my weak legs, my tired brown body, on.

Postscript

This collection began taking shape in the summer of 2015, though I didn't know it then. It was at this time that everything inside of me—all the experiences I have had related to my race and who I am as a person—began to blend together and patterns began to form before my eyes. The experience of that summer was just an echo of previous experiences, some having occurred as far back as when I was a child, but now taking different forms. It was also at this time when I began to see the world for what it really was.

To explain, I have grown up thinking and believing things to be one way but living another reality. I thought racism was something past and over with, something that happened before I was born. I thought men and women married whoever they wanted, that you liked who you liked because of who they were, that you loved them because of their soul. I thought that things like hair and skin and upbringing were just interesting attributes, fascinating things to admire, not reasons to hate or shun or ignore. I had no concept of "not enough" because everyone was enough. My awakening was rude and sudden and long overdue.

It was not until that summer that I realized my reality was not just sometimes different from what I believed of the world—but different altogether. Part of this was my relatively young age and deep naïveté, but part of it was a hopefulness that wanted things to be what I thought they were, not what they are. I didn't want to live in a world where the horrors I learned about in school and heard about from my parents and grandparents were still true. I didn't have to use a certain water fountain or step into the street when a white person walked by. I didn't have to learn in a segregated school; I had friends of different races and, mostly, I was unaware that I was different. So how could prejudice and racism still be alive? How could I be a victim of it?

It was before and during my last year as an undergraduate, in 2014, that I began to read authors of color more intentionally. Not just Black authors, but authors from around the world telling their different stories and presenting their different experiences. Instances of racism and prejudice were rampant in all of them. Jhumpa Lahiri's *Unaccustomed Earth* and Sherman Alexie's *The Absolutely True Diary of a Part-Time Indian* explored micro-aggressions and the small subtle ways the world breaks down the brown body and puts it in danger, systematically, culturally, and socioeconomically as Ta-Nehisi Coates also portrays in *Between the World and Me*. Toni Morrison spoke of the magic, the resilience, and the need for love of the Black body in *Beloved*.

In each of these novels I saw myself. I had experienced my own versions of those micro-aggressions, had experienced what I refer to as "the internal genocide" in my collection. They were never fatal wounds, but they weakened me all the same until I was mired in bitterness. Until then, I had not quite realized how much I was ambivalent about my body, but I was suddenly more aware of the push and pull of pride and disgust when I tried to love myself better through seemingly small but weighty acts like wearing my natural hair. I saw *white* and how it differed from the negativity of *brown*—the white lover, the white friend, the white world, in these novels. I saw the way whiteness projected hatred onto these characters, who then internalized that hatred and made it their own. I saw that whiteness was not better, but that *white just was* in America and we—myself and the characters and the authors—were marginalized.

Though they do not make an explicit appearance within the collection, the following novels have played a significant role in its creation as well:

Incidents in the Life of a Slave Girl by Harriet Jacobs, *Autobiography of an Ex-Colored Man* by James Weldon Johnson, *Passing* by Nella Larsen, and *A Lesson Before Dying* by Ernest J. Gaines. All have influenced the way I think about race in America and my own Blackness, subsequently framing the simultaneously jaded yet cautiously hopeful perspective from which I wrote this collection. Johnson's novel was especially poignant for me because, though I am not biracial, my family is as heavily mixed with white as his. Throughout the collection, I refer to my "white as silk" Creole grandmother, the lightness of my mother's skin, and most vividly, my hair. Three generations of women in my family have fought against scrutiny, confusion, prejudice, and deep disdain mainly due to how we look—the length of our hair, the hue of our skin—but also how we act. I could never "pass" like Johnson or the characters Irene and Clare in Larsen's *Passing*, but the narrative of the "tragic mulatto" in these novels is echoed throughout my childhood. It is a concept with which I am intimately familiar and which ricochets back to Du Bois' concept of double consciousness, the "two warring souls in one brown body" from *The Souls of Black Folk*, which I have used as a refrain and a motif throughout my work.

For me, the two warring souls are the soul of a

Black woman and a human soul. There are worldly attachments on my soul, elements that I won't carry with me into the next life, but which heavily influence my life here on Earth. I speak of how I felt and feel that I would be essentially be the same person no matter what race I was. This is to say that, for most of my life, my race was secondary to me and my personhood. It was the realization that my race was primary to everyone else that sparked my change in perspective, that told me the world will see me as different than who I am.

This realization changed almost every aspect of my life: friendships, relationships, academics, and family. I fell into a rhythm of embracing my Blackness in a way I never had before, as well as fiercely protecting the person I have always been from the subtle jabs and overt blows of racism and prejudice in their many, many forms. This collection is something of a metamorphosis: it is me transforming from all the things I ever held inside. Like the caterpillar, all of this was always within me, lying dormant, until the moment it was time to come apart and put myself back together. But the change was and is painful—it is the total rending of an old self, becoming a mess of a new self, piecing together elements that were and are and are not yet. It has become clear that living this life at this time in America was always going to lead to a change. That no matter when I started, so long as I was Black and still living in the United States, this transformation was always imminent.

I write about heritage and tradition and celebration, about how these things are both stolen from Black people, but also held closely by us as well. I cannot reconcile the evil and the destruction, but I can celebrate the utter strength of my people. We do not know exactly where we came from, but we made ourselves a home, a culture, a life. Like nature, we cannot be broken down. Others may try to cut us, burn us, remove us, tame us, wound us, or kill us, but in time we always rise, flourish and bloom. Despite the wounds, the manipulation, the despair, we *go on*. I wish there was less disillusionment, heartbreak, and pain, but that would mean less joy.

I speak to God throughout this collection, both wailing and praising. He is woven into the fabric of each piece because this is also my relationship to the Father in real life. He is parent and savior, teacher and friend. He holds my anger and my pain, listens to my questions about the things I feel I will never truly understand. Through my disillusionment He reminds me that there is much I do not know, giving me the peaceful rest that comes from unencumbered trust.

At the start of this collection, I had an idea of where I wanted to go and what I wanted to say, but the finished product is much more personal than I had planned or wanted. Sometime in the summer of 2015, there was a moment I can now point to and say, *There. That is where everything came together and fell apart.* Today, I am at once the same person I was before this collection took shape, and also a completely different person, which is to say that I am still the same naïve child who sees the world through a hopeful lens, what it could be rather than what it is, while at the same time I am also older and wiser and sadder and more fatigued. I feel I have just begun to make sense of the things that hurt— of the pieces that will never sit comfortably in my soul.

In this way, my collection feels like a child and

its completion like the finality of birth. It is out in the world now and I can hardly control where it goes from here, or how exactly it will grow. It is a living thing separate from me, but always connected to me. It will be read and interpreted a number of ways, and it will reflect me, but also speak to readers apart from me. I thank you, reader, for engaging not just my work, but my soul. I hope that here at the end you can walk away with a deeper of understanding of the beautiful, mean world and how it hurts and loves the brown body.

Acknowledgments

Ghost World 3 – Disillusionment first appeared in *The Amethyst Review* in Spring 2018, published online.

Defiance first appeared in *Neutrons Protons: A Journal of Literary Humor and Comics* in Fall 2014, published online.

Erasure first appeared in *Linden Avenue Literary Journal* in Spring 2018, published online.

Ghost World 1 – Heritage first appeared in *Spry Literary Journal* in Winter 2019, published online.

Hair first appeared in *Burnt Pine Magazine* in Spring 2019, published online.

In the World Where I Do Not Exist first appeared in *Split Lip Magazine* in Fall 2016, published online.

Ghost World 2 – Womanhood first appeared in *Crack the Spine Literary Magazine* in Fall 2018, published online.

Bibliography

Alexie, Sherman. *The Absolutely True Diary of a Part-Time Indian*. Little Brown, 2007.

Angelou, Maya. *And Still I Rise: A Book of Poems*. Random House, 1978.

DuBois, W. E. B. *The Souls of Black Folk*. Barnes & Noble Classics, 2005, pp. 3,9,155

Gaines, Ernest J. *A Lesson Before Dying*. Vintage Books, 1993.

Holiday, Billie, and Abel Meeropoll. "Strange Fruit." Commodore, 1939.

Jacobs, Harriet. *Incidents in the Life of a Slave Girl*. Barnes & Noble Classics, 2005.

Johnson, James Weldon. *The Autobiography of an Ex-Colored Man*. Barnes & Noble Classics, 2007.

Lahiri, Jhumpa. *Unaccustomed Earth*. Vintage Books, 2009.

Morrison, Toni. *Beloved*. Random House, 1987.
Ovid. *The Metamorphosis*. Barnes & Nobel Classics, 2005, pp. 24-32.

Root, George Frederick & Woolston, Clare Hurston, "Jesus Loves the Little Children (formerly known as "Tramp, Tramp, Tramp, The Boys Are Marching")," Civil War Song, 1864.

Ross, Kathryn. "Defiance," *Neutrons, Protons: A Journal of Literary Humor and Comics*, 2014.

Ross, Kathryn. "In the World Where I Do Not Exist," *Split Lip Magazine*, October 2016.

Ross Kathryn, "Erasure," *Linden Avenue Literary Journal*, May 2018.

Ross, Kathryn, "Ghost World 3 – Disillusionment,"

The Amethyst Review, May 2018.

Ross, Kathryn, "Ghost World 2 – Womanhood,"
Crack the Spine Literary Magazine, November
2018.

Ross, Kathryn, "Ghost World 1 – Heritage,"
Spry Literary Journal, January 2019.

Ross, Kathryn, "Hair," *Burnt Pine Magazine*, March
2019.

Editor's Note

This is a book of echoes, at once a path through a pain-shrouded past and a map toward a future where healing is possible. But first, as Kathryn tells both versions of herself in "Erasure," we must look at what we have been too afraid to examine. We must slow down and consider the wounds, opened and reopened for centuries, that create the world where these words were framed and formed. We must listen with no other intent but to grieve and allow that sadness to reshape us.

There was a moment in the editing process when, like stopping on a long hike to look back on the expanse of trail one has covered, I paused to reflect on the scope of the work being done in these pages. Rather, I was brought up short by these lines:

> "…but this is not helplessness. It is weight. I sit constant beneath the knowledge that there is little to be done—that to try would be to strain against centuries upon centuries of strivings turned to death turned to mourning turned to moaning ghosts hurling their laments from the broken boughs of ancient trees."

Black Was Not A Label is a reckoning of the most intimate nature that demands—gently but persistently— to be read more than once. The first passage through these lines is personal, a shared space between you and the author's experiences. But the return trip is where you will begin to hear the call and response of these separate passages now collected as one volume.

Pay attention to the way these words move like spirits to connect the weight and strain of our past to move through soul-deep hurt toward a hope that remains even still.

About the Editor

Michael Dean Clark is an associate professor of writing at Azusa Pacific University specializing in fiction, literary nonfiction, and digital literature. Co-editor of *Creative Writing in the Digital Age* and *Creative Writing Innovations* (Bloomsbury Academic), his creative work has appeared most recently in *Bull & Cross, The Windhover Journal, The Other Journal, Pleiades, and Angel City Review* among others.

Follow him on Twitter @MDeanClark or visit his website michaeldeanclark.com.

About the Author and Artist

Kathryn H. Ross is a writer, reader, and storyteller from sunny Southern California where she lives with her family and two cats. She earned her Bachelor's and Master's degrees in English and Writing from Azusa Pacific University in 2015 and 2018 respectively, and works as a copywriter and editor. Her writing focuses on everything from her relationship with God, faith, and spirituality to memory and sense of being, human connection and relationships, and the reality of Blackness as inherent otherness in America.

As a writer and person, Ross desires to get to the heart of relationships, stories, and people by stripping away the surface layers through contemplation, conversation, and time to reveal the inner soul. Read the rest of her creative works at speakthewritelanguage.com.

Originally published by PRONTO and designed
by Trevor Kaiser Allred

CPSIA information can be obtained
at www.ICGtesting.com
Printed in the USA
JSHW020806270123
36823JS00011B/78